The Race to Ross

JANET LORIMER

GLOBE FEARON
Pearson Learning Group

DOUBLE FASTBACK® SPY BOOKS

Against the Wall	The Last Red Rose
The Black Gold Conspiracy	Picture of Evil
Claw the Cold, Cold Earth	The Puppeteer
A Dangerous Game	**The Race to Ross**
Escape From East Berlin	The Silver Spy

Cover © Royalty-Free/Corbis. All photography © Pearson Education, Inc. (PEI) unless specifically noted.

Copyright © 2004 by Pearson Education, Inc., publishing as Globe Fearon®, an imprint of Pearson Learning Group, 299 Jefferson Road, Parsippany, NJ 07054. All rights reserved. No part of this book may be reproduced or transmitted in any form or by any means, electronic or mechanical, including photocopying, recording, or by any information storage and retrieval system, without permission in writing from the publisher. For information regarding permission(s), write to Rights and Permissions Department.

Globe Fearon® and Fastback® are registered trademarks of Globe Fearon, Inc.

ISBN 0-13-024631-X
Printed in the United States of America
1 2 3 4 5 6 7 8 9 10   07 06 05 04 03

1-800-321-3106
www.pearsonlearning.com

Bonnie Price looked carefully at her reflection in the small mirror. She patted a stray blond curl into place and checked her makeup. In a few minutes her plane would be landing and she wanted to look her best when she saw Ross.

Ross Carter! Bonnie still couldn't believe how much one man had changed her life.

Just eight months ago Bonnie had moved from her parents' home in San Francisco to her own apartment in Los Angeles. She'd had only one goal then—to become an actress.

Soon after she'd moved to Los Angeles, she'd gotten a job in a little flower shop near her apartment in Inglewood. Then she'd joined a little theater group. The actors in the group put on plays for schools and youth groups. They didn't get paid for their work, but it was good experience.

Bonnie knew that one day the experience could lead to something bigger. Maybe she'd get hired to do TV commercials. Or maybe she'd get a small part in a movie. That could lead to bigger parts. Bonnie loved to daydream about her future. She was determined to work as hard as she could toward her goal.

Then she'd met Ross. He did the bookkeeping at the flower shop. Mr. Tanaka, the owner, had introduced Ross to her.

Bonnie liked Ross from the moment she'd met him. He was a good-looking man, tall and dark-haired, with a good sense of humor.

He had moved to Los Angeles about the same time Bonnie had. Because they were both newcomers, they did a lot of sightseeing together. They explored everything, from Disneyland to the Sunset Strip. They rode the merry-go-round in Griffith Park, toured Universal Studios, and ate fresh enchiladas on Olivera Street. There was so much to see and do in southern California. They knew they would never get tired of living in this exciting place.

Little by little their friendship turned to romance. Ross was everything Bonnie had ever dreamed of finding in a man. He was gentle and kind and very supportive of her goals. When he'd asked her to marry him, Bonnie had felt very, very fortunate.

Of course there were a couple of things about Ross that puzzled Bonnie. For example, he seemed uneasy in crowds of people. Every now and then Bonnie would catch him looking nervously over his shoulder. When she asked him if something was wrong, he quickly changed the subject.

Another thing that puzzled her was Ross's reluctance to talk about his past. Bonnie had no idea where he'd lived before he moved to Los Angeles. She didn't know where he'd worked, or who his friends had been. He told her once that he didn't have a family. When he said it, he sounded so unhappy and bitter that Bonnie didn't ask what had happened to them. She hoped that in time he'd open up on his own and tell her about his past.

When Bonnie got off the plane, she saw that the terminal was filled with people. On Friday night, when Ross had dropped her at the airport, they had arranged to meet at the baggage area this afternoon. Bonnie made her way through the crowd and stood by the luggage carousel. Ross wasn't there yet. She looked around eagerly, hoping to catch sight of him in the crowd. She wasn't too concerned. He might have been caught in traffic. Or, maybe he was still hunting for a place to park.

Bonnie glanced at her watch. She had been waiting for 15 minutes, and there was still no sign of Ross. It wasn't like him to be late.

Thirty more minutes went by. Bonnie was beginning to wonder if something had happened to Ross. Maybe he'd gotten sick and couldn't come to pick her up. She decided she'd better phone him.

She found a pay phone nearby and dialed his number. She let the phone ring a dozen times, but there was no answer. Bonnie frowned. Now she was beginning to worry. She decided she wouldn't wait any longer. As Bonnie left the terminal she couldn't convince herself that nothing was wrong. She had a bad feeling that something was *very* wrong.

Bonnie took a taxi to her apartment. It was closer to the airport than Ross's apartment. From there, she planned to drive her own car out to the San Fernando Valley where Ross lived.

When she walked into her living room, she saw that the light was blinking on her answering machine. That meant that someone had tried to reach her while she was in San Francisco. Maybe it was Ross.

She rewound the tape and played it back. Sure enough, she heard Ross's familiar voice. "Hi, Bonnie, this is Ross. I just wanted to let you know that I've ordered the flowers for our wedding from Gino's."

Bonnie frowned. What in the world was Ross talking about? She rewound the tape and played the message back a second time. It still made no sense. She and Ross had already ordered their wedding flowers through Mr. Tanaka. She didn't even know anyone named Gino. Why had Ross left such a strange message? She replayed the tape a few more times, hoping that she'd make some sense of it. But she still couldn't figure it out.

Finally Bonnie reached for the phone and dialed Ross's number again. There was still no answer. Now she was beginning to get a very uncomfortable feeling in the pit of her stomach. There was no use sitting here, trying to find the answers. She grabbed her car keys and headed out the door.

The Sunday afternoon traffic wasn't as bad as she had feared it would be. But by the time she reached Ross's apartment, Bonnie was feeling very tense. She hurried into the building and knocked on Ross's door. No answer. She went down the hall and knocked on the manager's door. The man was just sitting down to eat his dinner.

Bonnie apologized for bothering him. When she explained her problem, he was more than willing to help. He agreed to let her into Ross's apartment.

"Come to think of it," he said, as he got his master keys, "I don't think I've seen Ross all weekend."

"All weekend?" Bonnie said. "But he told me he was planning on spending a quiet weekend here at home."

The manager shrugged. "All I know is, I saw him drive away late Friday night and I haven't seen him since. And his parking stall is still empty."

"What time did he drive away?" Bonnie asked.

The manager thought for a moment. "I'm not sure of the exact time, but I know it was after nine."

That meant that Ross had come home after dropping her at the airport and then gone out again. But gone where?

When the manager opened Ross's front door, Bonnie hurried into the apartment, calling his name. But there was no answer.

She quickly searched the other rooms, but it was clear that Ross was not there. When she reached the bedroom, Bonnie opened the closet door. For a moment she just stared in disbelief at the empty clothes hangers. Most of Ross's clothes were gone. So was his big suitcase.

Suddenly her knees felt weak and rubbery. She sat down on the edge of the bed, fighting back tears. Had Ross deserted her? Was it possible that he'd had second thoughts about marrying her? Had he come back to the apartment, packed a suitcase, and just disappeared so he wouldn't have to go through with the wedding?

Then common sense took over. That would not explain the strange message on her answering machine. No, there had to be another reason for his sudden departure.

"Excuse me," the manager said, sticking his head around the door. "If you don't mind, I'm going to get back to my dinner. You can stay here as long as you like. Just lock the front door when you leave."

Bonnie rubbed her eyes quickly to wipe away the tears. "Thanks," she said in a shaky voice. "I think I'd like to stick around awhile. Maybe Ross will be back soon."

The manager nodded and started to leave. Then he turned back. "Hey, don't worry," he said. "Something probably came up and he had to take off suddenly. You know, maybe someone in his family got sick or something."

Bonnie nodded and thanked the man. She knew he meant well. But if that was the reason Ross had left, why hadn't he just said so? Why had he left that strange message? Besides, he'd told her he had no family.

Bonnie heard the door close as the manager left. Now that she was alone in the apartment, she decided to search it. Maybe she'd find something that would tell her where Ross had gone. She went back to the living room and started to search his desk.

A sudden knock on the front door startled her. Bonnie looked at the door, puzzled. Ross had a key. So did the manager. So who could it be? She went to the front door and opened it.

A man Bonnie had never seen before was standing in the hallway. He looked like a businessman with his dark suit and tie. He seemed as surprised to see Bonnie as she was to see him.

"I'm looking for Ross Carter," the man said. "This is his apartment, isn't it?"

Bonnie nodded. "But he's not here right now," she said. "May I ask . . ."

The man reached into his pocket and pulled out a small leather folder. He opened it and held it up. Bonnie saw the badge and gasped.

"My name is Steve Channing," he said. "I'm with the FBI."

"The FBI?" Bonnie said in disbelief.

"May I come in?" Channing asked, putting his badge away. Bonnie nodded. She stood aside to let him enter.

"Why are you looking for Ross?" she asked, as Channing glanced around the small, neat living room.

"Mind if I ask your name first?" he said.

"Bonnie Price," she told him. "Ross and I are engaged to be married."

"Then you must know where he is," Channing said. "It's important that you tell me, Miss Price."

"Is Ross in some kind of trouble?" Bonnie asked.

Channing nodded. "I'm afraid so. But he's not in trouble with the law, if that's what you're thinking. I'm here to help him."

"Help him?" Bonnie asked. "How? Why?"

"Ross Carter is in a lot of danger," Channing said. "I want to find him so I can save his life."

"What are you talking about?" Bonnie cried. Her eyes widened with fear.

For a moment Channing was silent, studying her. Then he said, "Look, why don't we sit down. It's a long story."

After they were seated, he said, "First, does the name Warren Adams sound familiar?"

Bonnie nodded. "Yes, it does, but I don't seem to remember where . . ." She stopped, her eyes lighting up. "Wait a minute! Wasn't he some kind of spy?"

Channing nodded. "Warren Adams used to work for our government. Then, a little more than a year ago, we found out that he was stealing government secrets and selling them to a foreign power. Actually, Ross Carter was the one who first discovered what Adams was doing. You see, he worked in the same office with Adams. Carter's testimony was the evidence that convicted Adams. He received a life sentence. After the trial, Adams swore he'd kill Carter. So, to protect him, we put him in the Federal Witness Program."

"I've heard of that," Bonnie said.

"We gave Carter a new name and set him up here in Los Angeles with a whole new life."

"You mean Ross Carter isn't his real name?" Bonnie asked.

"That's right," Channing said.

"So that's why he never talked about his past," Bonnie murmured. "But with Adams in prison, Ross really wasn't in any more danger, was he?"

"He was in danger from the others," Channing said.

"What others?" Bonnie asked.

"We've always known that Adams wasn't working alone. He was the only one we caught, and we tried to get him to tell us who helped him. But he never did."

"And now you think that one of Adams's partners is trying to find Ross?" Bonnie asked.

"There's more to it than that," Channing said. "You see, Adams broke out of prison a few days ago. He was serving his time in a federal prison back east. At the moment we don't know where he is."

"But Adams doesn't know that Ross is here in Los Angeles, does he?" Bonnie asked. "Besides, you said Ross's name had been changed, too."

Channing nodded. "That's right. So we weren't really worried about Ross until Friday. Then something happened."

"What was it?" Bonnie asked, leaning forward, her hands tightly clasped together.

"Ross phoned me Friday night," Channing said. "He was very upset. He said he'd dropped you off at the airport and was heading back to his car. All of a sudden he heard someone call him by his old name."

"Was it Adams?" Bonnie gasped.

Channing shook his head. "No, according to Ross, it didn't sound like his voice. It could have been one of the others, someone who'd worked with Adams to steal those secrets. I tried to get Ross to stay put until I could get some men out here. But he wouldn't listen. I'm afraid he's trying to deal with this by himself. I think he's gone into hiding somewhere. The trouble is, I don't know how safe he is. I want to find him to make sure he's got proper protection."

Bonnie stared at Channing in horror. It hardly seemed possible that just a few hours ago she'd been so happy. Suddenly her world had turned upside down.

Channing leaned forward, his grey eyes filled with worry. "Please, Miss Price, if you have any idea where Ross might be, you've got to tell me."

Bonnie could only shrug helplessly. She explained that she'd been gone all weekend. "I just got back a few hours ago," she said. "When Ross didn't meet me at the airport, I began to worry. That's why I'm here. But I don't know where he is. Believe me, I'd tell you if . . ." Suddenly she stopped.

"What is it?" Channing asked.

"I've just remembered something," Bonnie said. "I don't know if it will help you. Ross left a very odd message on my answering machine. It makes no sense!"

"What is it?" Channing asked.

Bonnie told him. Then she added, "But we've already ordered our wedding flowers through our boss, Mr. Tanaka. So I can't figure out why he said that."

"You're right," Channing said. "It is strange. It sounds like Ross was trying to tell you something. Who is Gino, a friend of yours?"

"I don't know anyone by that name," Bonnie said. "And I can't figure out why Ross would leave that kind of message in the first place. Why didn't he just say what he meant? I don't have a roommate. He'd know that no one else would hear the tape but me."

Channing shrugged. "It is puzzling," he said. "Look, can you think of anything else that might help me? Anything at all? It's really important."

"No, nothing else," Bonnie said.

Channing sighed. "Well, thanks anyway. If you do hear from Ross again, or if you figure out that message, please call me right away." He wrote his phone number on a piece of paper and handed it to her. "Remember, his life is at stake. Call me day or night."

Bonnie took the paper and put it in her purse. "I'll call you if I think of anything that might help," she said. "I just hope Adams is recaptured before he finds Ross."

"So do I," Channing said grimly.

After Channing had gone, Bonnie turned out the lights and left the apartment. As night came to Los Angeles, she drove back down the San Diego Freeway to her apartment. And for the first time since she'd moved to this city, the bright lights failed to catch her attention. She was too deep in thought to notice their beauty.

When Bonnie got back to her apartment, she fixed herself a light supper and got ready for bed. She knew she had to get some rest. She had to be at work early in the morning. But she couldn't sleep. She was tense, listening for the phone to ring, hoping Ross would call.

Finally, after nearly an hour, she fell into a restless sleep.

Bonnie awoke suddenly, with a loud cry. The phone was ringing! Was it Ross? She reached over to the night table to pick it up. Then she realized it wasn't the phone at all. It was only her alarm clock. She shut off the alarm, and went to take a hot shower to wake herself up.

Bonnie had just finished getting dressed when she heard a loud knock on her front door. She hurried to answer it, hoping it was either Ross or Steve Channing to tell her that Ross was safe.

But when she opened the door, she found a strange woman standing in the hall. She was dressed in a navy blue suit and wore her brown hair in a neat bob.

"Bonnie Price?" the woman asked. Bonnie nodded. "My name is Laura Anderson. I'm with the FBI." She showed Bonnie her badge.

"Please come in," Bonnie said eagerly. "I hope you have good news. Is Ross safe? Has Warren Adams been captured?"

Laura stared at Bonnie in surprise. "How did you know we were looking for Ross Carter?" she asked.

"Steve Channing told me," Bonnie said.

"Steve Channing! You've seen Channing? Here? In Los Angeles?"

Bonnie nodded. "I saw him last night. Why? Is something wrong?"

"I'm afraid so," Laura said. "Tell me where you saw him and what he told you."

Bonnie told Laura the whole story. The woman began to pace up and down the room. "This is very bad news," she muttered. "I'd hoped that—" She stopped and faced Bonnie. "I think you should know that Steve Channing isn't what he claims to be."

"You mean he's not an FBI agent?" Bonnie said.

"Oh, he's an agent, all right. But we think he may be one of the inside people who worked with Adams to steal those government secrets. Channing has been under investigation within the agency for some time. Unfortunately, we haven't been able to prove it. However, before Adams went to prison, he threatened to talk. We think that Channing may have helped Adams escape from prison to keep him from naming names."

"If that's true," Bonnie said, "why would Channing want to find Ross?"

"We're pretty sure that Channing planned to kill Adams after he got him out of prison. But we think that Adams got away from Channing. If we're right, Channing needs to find Ross to bait a trap for Adams. After all, Adams would do anything to get his hands on Ross. Of course, if Channing's plan works, he'll kill both Adams and Ross. That's the only way he can protect himself."

"Oh, no!" Bonnie groaned, burying her face in her hands. "I may have helped Channing without meaning to."

"How?" Laura asked.

Bonnie told her about the strange message Ross had left on her answering machine. "It made no sense to me," she said. "But I told Steve Channing about it last night. He said he didn't know what it meant either, but if he manages to figure it out . . . " Her voice trailed off into silence. "I may have put Ross in even more danger," Bonnie added in a shaky voice.

Laura stared at Bonnie with a puzzled frown. "It certainly is an odd message," she said. "Are you sure Ross didn't say anything else?"

"Nothing," Bonnie said. "That was the whole message."

"And you haven't heard from him since?"

Bonnie shook her head.

Laura stood up. "Well I have to go, Bonnie, but here's my phone number. If you do figure out that message, let me know right away."

Bonnie nodded. "I will."

"And if you hear from Ross, don't try to act on your own. Call me first. Okay?"

"Well . . ." Bonnie said slowly.

"Listen," Laura said, "Channing may be following you, hoping you'll lead him right to Ross. It could be very dangerous for both you and Ross if you try something on your own."

Bonnie shivered. "I'll do what you say," she promised.

After Laura left, Bonnie grabbed her purse and car keys and headed for the flower shop. When she arrived, a little while later, Mr. Tanaka was already at work. He was turning a plain bunch of daisies into a beautiful floral arrangement. When he saw her, he smiled. "I was getting worried about you," he said. "I was afraid you and Ross had decided to elope!"

Usually her boss's teasing made Bonnie laugh, but not today. "I'm afraid I have bad news about Ross," she said.

Mr. Tanaka saw the worried expression on Bonnie's face. He put down the wire he was holding. "What's wrong, Bonnie?"

"Everything!" she burst out. She told him all that happened since the day before. "I should never have accepted Steve Channing at face value," she said bitterly. "I should have called the FBI to double-check on him. I should have—"

"Stop blaming yourself," Mr. Tanaka said. "It's not your fault, Bonnie."

"But if Channing figures out that message, then Ross may be killed," she said.

"Then we'll just have to figure it out before Channing does," Mr. Tanaka said. "Tell me again what Ross said."

Bonnie repeated the message while Mr. Tanaka wrote it down. He stared at the paper for a long time. Suddenly a funny look came over his face. "Say that name again."

"Gino's," Bonnie said. "It sounds like a place that sells pizza, not flowers."

"Wait a minute!" Mr. Tanaka said excitedly. "It's not Gino's, Bonnie. It's Gene O's." He wrote the two words on the paper to show her the difference.

"Does that name mean something to you?" Bonnie asked.

Mr. Tanaka grinned and nodded. "Oh, yes, Bonnie. If it's what I think it is, we may have figured out what Ross was trying to tell you—and where he's hiding."

Bonnie gazed at her boss with growing excitement. "Tell me!"

"Gene O is a nickname for a man in New York," Mr. Tanaka said. "His full name is Gene Owens. He's a flower wholesaler. He sells flowers to flower shop owners around the country like me. Gene deals in very rare flowers and plants. For example, if I need orchids in December, I get in touch with him."

"Gene Owens," Bonnie said slowly. "Do you suppose that Ross knows him? Ross never talked about his past. I don't even know where he lived before he came to Los Angeles."

"I'm sure Ross knows Gene," Mr. Tanaka said. "And I'll tell you how I know that. One afternoon a few months ago, Ross and I were going over my accounts. Ross came across an invoice from Gene. He pointed to the name and he asked if I knew the man. I told him that I had done business with Gene Owens for years. I said I didn't know much about him outside of the business, but I had always found him to be very pleasant and honest to deal with."

"What did Ross say?" Bonnie asked.

"Ross nodded. Then he said something like, 'Yeah, Gene's a good guy,'" Mr. Tanaka said.

Bonnie's eyes sparkled with excitement. "Ross *must* know him," she said. "And that's what he was trying to tell me! I bet Ross has gone to New York. Maybe Gene Owens knows where he is."

Mr. Tanaka nodded eagerly. "Yes, Bonnie, that must be the answer. Here!" He shoved the phone toward her. "Call

Gene and tell him what's happened. Tell him Ross must be warned."

He gave Bonnie the number. She dialed it as quickly as her shaking fingers would let her. When a woman answered, Bonnie asked to speak to Gene Owens. In a moment her eager smile vanished, and she hung up.

"He's not in his office," she told Mr. Tanaka. "His secretary doesn't know when he'll be back. I didn't dare leave a message. I want to speak directly to Mr. Owens."

"I agree," Mr. Tanaka said. "But you've got to keep trying to reach him, Bonnie. Go back to your apartment. Maybe Ross will try to call you. But if not, keep trying to reach Gene."

"I can't do that," Bonnie said. "There's too much work here at the shop."

Mr. Tanaka smiled. "Please, Bonnie. You have so much on your mind today, that I'm afraid you'll end up cutting off the blossoms instead of trimming the stems! No, this is much too important. You go home."

Bonnie smiled, too. Her boss was probably right. She'd never be able to concentrate on her work. She thanked Mr. Tanaka for his concern, picked up her things, and left the shop.

Twenty minutes later Bonnie was back home. As soon as she walked in the door, she decided to phone Gene Owens again. She reached for the phone and started to dial. Then she was struck with a new thought, one that sent chills down her spine.

Was it possible that Ross had been so mysterious because he was afraid her phone might be tapped? Bonnie dropped the receiver as if it were a poisonous snake. She stared at it in mistrust. Was she being foolish? Had she seen too many spy movies to think calmly and coolly? Or were her fears right on target? After all, as an FBI agent, Steve Channing would know how to tap into her line. And if he were an agent who had gone bad, he would stop at nothing to find Ross.

She put the receiver back on its hook. She could use her cell phone, but hadn't she read that cell phones are even less private? Somebody could easily be sitting outside right now picking up her signals. Bonnie paced up and down the room. She felt trapped.

She glanced at the clock and saw that it was almost time for the hourly television news update. Maybe there would be some news of the Warren Adams case. She switched on the TV and settled herself on the couch.

Sure enough, the Adams case was the lead story. Because Adams hadn't been caught, and because he'd been labeled a dangerous fugitive, the story was still hot. There were even some old film clips of Adams after his trial.

Bonnie shivered a little as she watched the film. Adams had wild eyes and an ugly smile. He looked dangerous and unstable. As he was being led away after the trial, the reporters tried to close in around him to ask him questions.

Bonnie noticed that there was a woman with Adams, but the crowd of reporters blocked Bonnie's view of her. Bonnie could see that Adams had his arm around the woman's shoulder and she guessed that this might be Adams's wife. Then the narrator named the woman. She was Lola Adams, Warren's sister.

Suddenly, the woman turned and glared at the camera. Her face was streaked with tears, and she was obviously upset. Bonnie gasped and sat bolt upright. It wasn't the woman's anger that shocked Bonnie, it was her *face!* This was the same woman who, just a few hours before, had come to see Bonnie! Bonnie knew her as Laura Anderson, the FBI agent!

Bonnie stared blindly at the TV screen as the truth began to sink in. She'd been fooled again. Laura

Anderson was really Lola Adams. She had only been pretending to be an FBI agent. And Bonnie had trusted her. It had never occurred to Bonnie that Lola could have deceived her just the way Channing had. She had trusted the woman, and believed her, completely. Bonnie was so angry at herself she wanted to scream.

Then a new thought crossed her mind. Had Lola Adams *lied* about Steve Channing? Was he really what he'd said he was, an FBI agent trying to find Ross to protect him? Or was he trying to find Ross to kill him?

Bonnie realized she could not trust either one of them. And one fact remained. Both Lola and Steve now had that message. So Ross was in danger from one or the other—or both. He had to be warned, and Bonnie could think of only one way to warn him. She had to find him herself.

Bonnie ran into the bedroom and pulled her suitcase from the closet. She started to throw clothes into it, when she suddenly realized she'd come close to making another bad mistake. If she were being watched and followed, she could be leading the enemy straight to Ross.

Bonnie dropped the dress she was holding and sat down on the edge of the bed. She felt helpless. She had to get to Ross and warn him, but she couldn't use the phone or leave the apartment. Then what *could* she do?

Bonnie glanced over at her dressing table. On it were several bottles and jars of makeup. *Makeup!* Of course! Bonnie realized that she could disguise herself so no one following her would ever recognize her.

This idea brought her fresh hope. But this time when Bonnie began to sort through her clothes, she did so with great caution. She remembered the fun she'd recently had designing a witch's costume for a local production of *Macbeth* she'd been in. Yes, that had been fun. But this role would be played very seriously. Bonnie took a deep breath. There was so much at stake. Ross's life might depend on her ability to get out of town without being followed.

A half-hour later, Bonnie's disguise was complete. She carefully examined her reflection in the mirror. Every detail had to be perfect. At last she was satisfied. Pretty, young Bonnie Price had disappeared. In her place stood a plain-looking woman in her early forties, with mousy brown hair, wearing a drab suit, and thick glasses.

Bonnie collected only a few things she needed to take with her. She took things that could easily be stuffed into her large purse. She wanted to look like an ordinary woman going shopping.

After she was sure she was ready, Bonnie left the apartment. She caught the bus at the corner and rode it to a nearby shopping center. From there she took a taxi to the airport. She hoped that if anyone had seen her leave, they hadn't recognized her.

When she reached the airport, Bonnie bought a ticket for the first available flight to New York. She still wasn't certain that Ross *was* in New York. But she knew that was where Gene Owens was. And she hoped if she could find him, he'd lead her to Ross.

When Bonnie boarded the plane, she settled into her seat and allowed herself to relax. She was able to sleep a little from time to time on the long flight. But she did not feel rested when the plane finally landed. Her eyes felt gritty with exhaustion. She hoped that in a few hours this nightmare would be over.

She found a pay phone in the terminal and dialed Gene Owens's number. "Please let him be in his office," she said to herself.

"Gene Owens!" a voice said on the other end.

Bonnie took a deep breath. "Mr. Owens, my name is Bonnie Price," she began nervously.

"Bonnie Price!" His voice was filled with surprise. "Ross Carter's Bonnie?"

"Yes," she said, relieved that he recognized her name.

"Where are you calling from?" he asked.

"Here. New York. I'm at the airport. You see—"

"You're in New York?" he asked in disbelief.

"Yes, Mr. Owens. I've got to talk to you about Ross. You see—"

"Wait a minute!" he said abruptly. "Before you go on. I want to ask you a question. On your first date with Ross, he took you out to dinner. He ordered a steak and you had shrimp. How was the shrimp prepared?"

"What?" She couldn't believe what she was hearing.

"You say you're Bonnie Price," Owens said. "If so, you know the answer to the question."

"B-but you've got it all wrong," she stammered, her eyes filling with tears. "I didn't order shrimp. I can't eat shrimp. I'm allergic to it."

Gene Owens chuckled. "Okay, you're Bonnie Price. Sorry for the trick question. But I had to be sure. By the way, you're the only thing Ross has talked about in the last few days."

Bonnie almost sobbed with relief. "I've missed him terribly," she said. "Is he all right? I've been worried sick. You see, Ross is in terrible danger, and it's all my fault and—"

"Slow down," Gene told her. "Start at the beginning."

Bonnie told him everything that had happened. He listened without interrupting. At last he said, "Bonnie, do you realize that you may have been followed?"

"I don't think so," she said, and she quickly described her disguise.

"Ross told me you were a terrific actress," he said. "Good thinking, Bonnie."

"Mr. Owens, I've got to get to Ross," Bonnie said. "I have to warn him!"

"Take it easy," Gene said. "I don't want to talk about this over the phone. I'll pick you up in front of the terminal." Then he described himself and the van he'd be driving.

Bonnie recognized Gene Owens the moment she saw him. He was a big, burly man with a dark beard that made him look a little like a pirate. But his eyes twinkled and he had a wide grin.

As they pulled away from the curb, Gene said, "It's a good thing you told me about that disguise. I wouldn't have known who you were."

Bonnie laughed. "Let's hope the enemy didn't recognize me either. Seriously, though, I'm sure I wasn't followed. And that's why I have to get to Ross. Before it's too late. If Steve or Lola figure out that message—"

Gene frowned. "Bonnie, I know how much you want to see Ross. But I'm not so sure it's a good idea. The fewer people who know where Ross is hiding, the safer he'll be."

"But if Steve or Lola have already figured out that message, they may be in New York right now. In fact, isn't it possible that they might have followed you to Ross's hiding place?"

"I hadn't thought about that," Gene said grimly. "All right, I'll take you to him. Let's just hope we aren't too late!"

On the way, Gene told Bonnie that Ross was hiding in a cabin in the mountains "It'll take awhile to get there," he added. "Why don't you try to relax and get some rest. You look exhausted. Or is that just part of the disguise?"

"No," Bonnie grinned. "I am tired, but I don't think I'll be able to sleep. I'm too excited and too worried about Ross."

But before she knew it, she'd dozed off. Suddenly she felt Gene shaking her arm. "Sorry to disturb your sleep," he told her, "but we're almost there."

Bonnie yawned, and stretched and sat up. They were on a highway that curved through the mountains. There were thick woods on each side of the road. "It's beautiful here," she said.

"It's always been a favorite place of mine," Gene said. "I like to get away from the city now and then. Look, I don't think we're being followed, but I wouldn't swear to it. So this is what I want you to do."

He explained that they would soon reach the dirt road that led to the cabin. "I'll slow down long enough for you to get out of the van. The moment you do, get into those trees as fast as you can. As soon as you're out of the van, I'll drive on. There's a place down the road where I can hide the van in the trees. Then I'll double back on foot."

Bonnie nodded, and got ready to jump out of the van when Gene slowed down. They rounded a curve in the road and he suddenly pulled over. "Now!" he said.

Bonnie jumped out of the van and ran into the trees. She heard the van pull away, and she was on her own. There was a dirt road that led through the woods, but Bonnie stayed on the very edge of it. She felt safer near the protection of the trees. She followed the road for about half a mile until she saw the cabin in a clearing just ahead.

She felt a sense of relief. At last! In a few moments she would be with Ross. Nothing else mattered as long as they were together. Forgetting her earlier fears, Bonnie broke into a run.

When she reached the cabin door, she turned around. She saw no one behind her. She breathed a sigh of relief and knocked on the cabin door. "Ross, it's me, Bonnie," she called out.

From inside she heard Ross's voice. "Come in, Bonnie." She threw open the door and burst into the cabin. Ross was standing near the fireplace. She ran into his arms, burying her face against his shoulder. "Oh, Ross, you don't know how glad I am to see you."

When he didn't answer, she pulled back and looked at him. He had a strange look on his face. And he wasn't looking at her, but at something across the room. Bonnie turned and saw a man and woman watching her. It was Warren Adams and his sister, Lola. And Lola was holding a gun.

Ross pulled her close to him again. "Bonnie, honey, what are you doing here?"

Bonnie's eyes filled with tears of anger and frustration. "I came to warn you," she said bitterly. "But I'm too late."

"Oh, I wouldn't say that," Lola laughed. "The fun is just about to begin. My goodness, Miss Price, if you hadn't announced yourself, I never would have recognized you. What a clever disguise!"

"I didn't want to be followed," Bonnie said to Ross. "Oh, Ross, this is all my fault. I'm afraid I helped this woman find you. I didn't mean to, but—"

"Oh, shut up, you two!" Warren Adams snapped. Then he grinned. "This is even better than I'd hoped, Lola. First I'll kill the girlfriend. Slowly. Then, this squealer over here," he said, pointing at Ross.

Ross pushed Bonnie behind him. "Can't you leave her out of this, Adams?" he said. "She never did anything to you."

"Don't be a fool!" Lola snapped. "She knows too much." Then she said to Warren, "I don't have time for your little cat-and-mouse games, Warren. I hadn't planned on having two bodies to get rid of. We have to—"

She stopped, as if suddenly listening to something. Then they all heard the sound of a car pulling into the clearing.

Warren tensed. "Who's that?" he hissed.

A moment later, Steve Channing stood in the doorway. He was holding a gun. Bonnie drew her breath in sharply, hopeful that Channing had come to rescue them. Then, to her horror, he walked over to Lola and Warren.

"Good work, Lola," he said.

Bonnie felt sick with fear. She and Ross didn't stand a chance. Then she remembered Gene. He was probably on his way to the cabin by now. And when he saw the cars in the clearing, he'd surely know something was wrong. Maybe she and Ross did stand a chance. If only she could buy some time.

But while she was trying to figure out what to do to stall for time, Channing suddenly shoved Warren Adams toward Ross and Bonnie. The man stumbled against Ross, almost knocking him over. Then he recovered his balance and whirled around. "What in blazes are you doing?" he roared to Channing.

Steve and Lola moved close together, their guns trained on the other three. "It's simple," Channing said. "We didn't break you out of prison just to keep you from talking, or to help you get even with Carter. There's something we want!"

"What?" Warren said.

"The money," Lola snapped. "We know the FBI never recovered your take of the money."

"You got paid your share," Warren said.

"But it wasn't enough, brother dear," Lola said. "We want it all!"

"I'm the one who took all the risks," Warren exclaimed. "I'm the one who went to prison. The rest of the money is mine."

Lola grinned. "If Steve and I hadn't figured out how to get you out of prison, you would have turned us over to the feds in a minute," she said. "Don't talk to us about risks, Warren. We took risks, too. No, this is a fair trade. You get Carter and the girl. We get the money and a chance to get out of the country.

"We've been planning this for a long time, Warren," Lola went on. "We have no intention of leaving here without knowing where the money is. So here's the deal. You tell us where you stashed your share.

We'll give you a gun. You'll have Carter and the girl and you can do what you like to them."

Warren just shook his head. "You're crazy! I'm not going to tell you a thing."

Channing shrugged. "Then I'm afraid you won't leave this cabin alive, Warren."

Warren Adams was almost babbling with rage. His eyes had a wild look, and Bonnie shivered, knowing he was on the very edge of madness.

Next to her, Ross tensed. Bonnie glanced at him and saw that he was looking at the open door. Did he think they could make a break for it? Bonnie knew they didn't have a chance of getting out the door alive. She glanced at the window. It was closer but . . .

Suddenly, through the window, she saw a flash of color in the clearing. Gene. He'd made it back to the cabin and he'd spotted the cars. He knew something was wrong and now he was sneaking up on the cabin. Bonnie took a deep breath. She had to think of a way to distract Lola and Channing long enough for Gene to make his move.

"Time's up, Warren," Lola snapped. "Tell us where the money is!"

"You . . . you . . ." Warren glared at Lola, his voice filled with hate. "You witch!" he screamed. "You'll pay for this!"

Witch! Bonnie took a deep breath. She knew what she had to do.

Lola raised the gun. "Last chance, brother," she sneered.

Suddenly the cabin was filled with an awful earsplitting cackle of laughter. Everyone jumped a foot. The next second a shot rang out. Lola screamed. Ross shoved Adams toward Channing and Lola. They were knocked over like bowling pins, their guns clattering to the floor.

"Everyone freeze!" Gene yelled from the doorway.

Ross hurried over to the tangle of bodies and picked up the guns. "On your feet!" he growled.

Gene told Bonnie that there was a phone in the bedroom. "Call the police," he said.

Much later, after the three spies had been taken away, Bonnie said, with relief, "I can't believe the nightmare is over. Oh, Ross, I was sure we were both going to be killed."

"If you hadn't scared them with that crazy laugh," Ross said, "we might have been killed. You saved us, sweetheart."

Gene laughed. "Definitely an academy award-winning laugh, Bonnie!"

"There are a couple things I still don't understand," Bonnie told Ross as they headed for Gene's van. "Just who was it that you saw at the airport Friday night? Steve or Lola?"

"Both of them," Ross said. "You see, they broke Warren out of prison and got him a safe hiding place. They knew they had to keep him from talking to the FBI. But they were greedy, too. They wanted the money that Warren had stashed away. They decided to use me as the bait. They'd give me to Warren in exchange for the money."

"And since Channing was an agent, he knew you were in Los Angeles," Bonnie said.

Ross nodded. "That's right. So they flew to Los Angeles to find me. But they didn't expect to see me at the airport. It was such a shock that Lola called me by my old name. When I saw the two of them together, all the pieces of the puzzle fell into place. I realized that Channing was one of Warren's partners. I managed to get away from them, and you know the rest."

"Not exactly," Bonnie said. "Why did Lola pretend to be working against Steve instead of with him?"

"Steve knew that the FBI really did suspect him of helping Adams steal the government secrets. He knew it was only a matter of time before the FBI sent another agent to see you, to tell you about him. So he and Lola decided to stay one step ahead of them. Lola pretended to be an agent. She also hoped that you would have figured out my message, or heard from me. Then you'd tell her where I was hiding."

"But I hadn't figured it out," Bonnie said.

"I know. Lola was very disappointed and frustrated. Then, by chance, she and Channing figured it out for themselves. They found Gene's name in my background file that Channing pulled from the FBI files. They knew I had worked for Gene years ago when I lived in New York. From the message you gave them, they figured Gene was the person I contacted when I disappeared. So they flew to New York and began following him. They found this place when he drove up here to bring me more groceries."

"Did Lola and Channing come up here separately?" Bonnie asked.

Ross nodded. "Lola brought her brother here alone to lure him into the trap. Channing was just waiting down the road a bit getting ready to make his move. But, before he did, you showed up."

Gene nodded. "Well now you two can get back to planning that wedding of yours. And by the way, I plan to be there."

Ross laughed. "Didn't I tell you? You're going to be the best man, buddy!"

"There's one thing you should know," Bonnie said. "I plan to make a small change in the ceremony."

"Oh?" Ross looked surprised. "What kind of a change?"

"I'm going to revise our wedding vows," Bonnie said firmly. "There's one part I want to change, a phrase that almost came true."

"What's that?" Ross asked.

Bonnie took a deep breath. "Till death do us part," she said.